Menhir

A poetic invocation of the Cornish landscape

Alex Langstone

Menhir

A poetic invocation of the Cornish landscape

Alex Langstone

With illustrations
by Paul Atlas-Saunders

Spirit of Albion Books

First published in 2017 by

Spirit of Albion Books, Cornwall, UK

www.spiritofalbionbooks.co.uk

ISBN 978-0-9563554-4-7

Front cover painting: *From Treslea*
© Paul Atlas-Saunders

All illustrations © Paul Atlas-Saunders

By the same author:

Bega and the Sacred Ring

Lucifer Bridge

Spirit Chaser

From Granite to Sea (coming soon...)

Alex Langstone, folklorist, poet and investigator of landscape mysteries, has been fascinated by the innumerable legends, myths and folklore of the Cornish landscape for much of his life. This collection is primarily inspired by and focused on the ideas and concepts of the *genius loci*, or spirit of place, and is influenced by various inspirational Cornish landscapes from across the Duchy. For details of Alex's work please see:

www.alexlangstone.com
www.cornishfolklore.co.uk

Contents

Buckator

Oh, Great Divine Spirit of
Land and sea
Feel the hum of the earth
And follow me
Through the deepest glen and
The darkest cave
The highest cliff and the
Biggest wave.

Androgynous One of
The portal deep
Who visits me
During restful sleep
Whirling swirling energy dances,
Spiralling round
From the turning tides below this
Sacred ground.

Buckator cliff top ancient land
Fire through the blood
Though once you were banned,
Serpentine power coursing through
The earth below
Visionary scenes to us
You may show.

Revealing the hidden, arcane and
The strange
The cosmic inspirer may send
Us deranged
Flowing through rivers,
Over land and through sea
Oh, Fair Buckator's secret,
Proclaim unto me.

This place of misrule twixt
Dark hills and the sea,
Where elemental creatures
May hold the key
To the mystic light from
The sun beyond dreams
Where again we find,
All is not as it seems!

Oh, Great Horned Bucka
Rides the wind and the waves,
Amongst the shadowy realm where
We tread the maze
Our intangible guide
On the crooked path,
Whose entrance maybe found
In the fiery hearth.

Joan the Wad

Deep within the shadows cast by the
Light of the billowing harvest moon
A green wispy flame
Is dancing along the ancient silvery
Illuminated secret pathways
That border the misty granite moor.

The green flame-like torch
A Faery incandescent glow that
Guides us 'cross the
Peaty bog, through rushes green
Shimmering in the
Gwynngala moonlight.

The invisible Queen
Liminal Joan, dances
Through the weave of time.
Veiled in sylvan silver light
Her torch illuminating
Her landscape of dreams

Where fantasies manifest
And all seems
Topsy-turvy
In the moonlight,
On the moor.

Hand maiden of Nature
Moonlit messenger
Torch-lit track ways,
Lined and guarded
By her Fae-folk, just a foot-fall away

Glistening, shimmering, glittering
Dancing by the snaking singing river
The flickering light of her torch
Safely guiding us through the
Eternal and ceaseless dream.

Pennkarow

Liminal movement
By the darkened hedge
From the threshold of night,
Floating in time
Branches dance,
Teased by the forest crown
Eyes peering from the
Dense blackness.
Something stirs
A quickening
There are no stars tonight
Just a low dense mist
Rising from the valley floor.

Solitary vistas give way to
The antlered red beast
As he leaps over the ancient ramparts
Into my path.
Time slows, eyes meet

Infinite possibilities tonight on
The hilltop settlement of
The ancient ancestors.
He quickly disappears again
Heading back into his
Woodland realm
Continuing his solitary
Journey to the river.

Bronn Wennili

On the highest hill
Where the old ones lie, watching over
The vast and remote land
Of old Foweymoor, herself
Secured by ghosts of the
Distant past
And the dancing murmurations,
Which suddenly manifest aloft like a
Wisht fog in the winter sky.

The ascent via the stones on the
Faerie fern acre valley floor,
Where the hills loom high
The circle is watched over by the old
Rocking stone upon Louden's
Lofty spine and
Roughtor's rocky crown where the
Temple room of Michael once sat
Between moulded granite forms.

Folk memory and history
Exude from this lofty peak,
The ridge backed silhouette
The roof of our peninsular land
Where hidden shrines and

Enigmatic barrows hint at
An untold story, hidden history
On the peak of this
Delectable moorland summit.

The granite highlands
In the northern reaches of the land
Bronn Wennili
Crowns the moor with
Graceful beauty and
Conjures the ancient Spirit of Place
Of the grand ascent
Atop the vast windswept uplands
Inspiring clarity of vision.

Brown Willy, Hill of Swallows
Inspirational and enchanting,
Dark and enticing
Your slopes of mystery lead us to
Explore your wondrous delectable
Contours along your rocky,
Spiny ridge, where distant coasts are
Sometimes glimpsed and mazed
Piskie beds loom from the peat below.

Idless

Stealthily they drop
To the ground
Hardly making any sound
By the Scrying Pool round
Whence hidden secretive
Energy abounds.

A still sheet of water
From on high
Reflecting the sun and
Stars and sky
The dragonflies dart, dancing by
Guarding the waters of prophecy.

The babbling of the
Woodland stream
Ushers us into a trance-like dream
Beneath the

Shimmering aspen trees
Staring into the mirror pool, we see…

Crystalline waters
Soft and still
Perfected vision is such a thrill
The softly spoken spirits came
They talked to and inspired
Us once again.

The running water gently sang
Of other existences
From whence we sprang
Tell me now,
Oh Sacred Stream
Where exactly have you been?

In these ancient woods on
The sacred land
Where the spirits gather,
We understand
Sacred Nature to whom we pray
We shall return to again one day.

Spring Equinox Meditation

As the light finally
Catches its
Twin faced dark
A brief truce is called
As the balance
Of opposites
Merge and entwine.

As new life emerges
From the
Cold dark earth
The egg of creativity
Breaks at the
Crack of dawn, and
The leaping hare dance.

As the rain and wind swirls
Around the budding branches
The sunset approaches,
And equinoctial
Balance allows the sun's rays

To burst through the bank
Of grey cloud.

The illuminating rays of the
Equinox sun
Allow the flowers to glow
As they dance in the whirling wind
Joyfully they nod to the
Descending fiery orb
Beyond the solitary towering oak.

Solstice

Dancing entwined across
The summer sky
Dragons dart flying,
Flying by
Undine serpent unfurls
And awaits, in the
Herby undergrowth lies the
Energy bait.

Rearing monsters from a
Slumbering sleep
Rise up and shine from the
Darkening deep,
Solstice sun through the
Dappled leaves
Serpent pulses, glistens
Then he takes his leave.

Dragons fused in
The summer sky
Above the ancient oak,
We hear their ancient cry
Mid-summer passions
Waft and wend
Through the rippling
Shade, to the shining end.

Secretive journeys
Through the slumbering hills
Entwining, colliding,
Taking their fill
Summer energy pulses,
Pulses round
To where it is needed and
There can be found.

Allantide Dreaming
A meditation

Crows crowing, flapping somewhere overhead. The wind cries the ghostly song of the departed. We stand alone in this dark, yet welcoming place. It is cold, and dusk is laying her blanket over the rolling landscape of sweeping, undulating hills. The naked twisted trees dance in the half light of a cold autumnal evening, and vicious clouds scud across a menacing sky. Old ossifying bones lie hidden here. The bone-yard of the ancient ones lie sleeping in this valley, and the ancient mortuary house holds the key to this place. Half buried under four thousand years of mud and stone. Whispers, half-forgotten whispers, from the dimming memory of yester-year.

Fading in and out, blending, melding 'twixt the winds playful movement 'neath the trees. We can almost taste the past here. Fleeting and unknowable, but tangible and contradictory. All of this and more. Scattered shards of invisible bone. Ghostly hair, tooth and nail hide here amongst the invisible remains of last years' decay. New life sprouts, mushrooming fungus and multi-coloured lichen have successfully colonised this enclosure.

This space, this sacred area of the deceased; the departed ones who haunt another realm, an inaccessible realm of half-fulfilled dreams and visions of poets and painters from across the ages. Ancient prehistoric lines of power converge here. The shining pathways of the ancestors, corpse roads and coffin paths where we may walk with the dead.

It is dark now, and the Yew tree observes all from the darkest corner of this enchanted world. This is the ancient, wise and cunning you.

Tree of departed souls, tree of renewal, guardian tree of graves. The old twisted branches rustling and creaking in the ghostly vale of dreams.

We find ourselves standing in the corner of a churchyard by a huge ancient tree. Its hollow trunk, gnarled and split with age, appears like a gateway leading us into the night. A crescent moon illuminates the darkened sky and the stars' glisten, communicating their history across time. This is a thin place. Allow yourself to be guided along the faintly illuminated old straight track, from the thousand-year-old Yew and its surrounding grave-stones, we walk along a well-defined path. This ancient corpse road follows an even older line of earth energy and it has a purposeful and meaningful destination.

An owl screeches and a rustling is heard in the nearby undergrowth.

Nocturnal creatures are busy. Old fashioned lanterns light our way towards the hill of the dreaming dead. Ancient standing stones pierce the landscape, and a wheel-headed wayside cross leads us to our destination. A bone-fire is burning on a hilltop. The assembly casting the bones of the Samhain feast into the blaze, remembering and honouring around a beacon fire, burning into the night's darkness, lighting a pathway into the dreamtime of the departed. But this is not our destination; we have a date with a more ancient edifice.

We continue along the faintly illuminated track-way leading us deeper into the starry, peaceful night. We walk through ancient woodland; the trees stand dark against the night. We are heading into Bone Valley. A deeply connected and primitive coombe. A place of antiquated trees and ancient secrets. Bone Valley will soon reveal our holy destination. The moon's crescent appears once more between the protruding branches, which seem to reach out to the darkness of night. The clouds have dispersed and bright stars shine like timeworn torches in an antique sky. Soon we arrive at a clearing and we see a stone structure, megaliths protruding from the earth. They are curbing a large oval mound and beyond the stones, through a well-worn entrance, we find a gaping black opening leading into a stone chamber. Some of the stones have been carved and circular indents cause the surface of one stone to stand out, its quartz veins glisten in the pale moonlight.

We sit within the confines of the barrow's heart, submerged within the silence. We light a solitary candle. We pray for the souls of our beloved departed, and if we so wish, we may speak with those who have left this world for the next.

We emerge from the otherworldly chamber of the Neolithic shrine of the dead. It is dawn, and the eastern sky is glowing an iridescent red. The sun is rising, lighting our way home. We follow the pathway back to the source of our dreamtime pilgrimage. Past the bone-fire hill, along the old straight track which leads through the heart of the November woods and past the ancient Yew. We take leave of this place, with its needles of stone and its earthy shrines of the dead. We once again find ourselves in a churchyard, amongst the gravestones, and then at home, amid the safety and comfort of our own world, with the illuminated turnip lanterns and bright red apples of the Cornish feast of Allantide.

Golitha

Here at this ravishingly spectacular
Emerald-green ravine
Where the Fowey tumbles
Noisily toward the
Pungent saliferous sea
Hoary Oak and Beech
Cling to the vertical
Ghost-ridden glen
Where glimpses of Doniert
And the *Pobel Vean* of the woods
Can be seen on moonlit nights
Flitting between tree and river.

In this illustrious ancient place
This entrancing singing waterfall
Bubbling, frothy, foamy
White water
Cascading, boiling and exuberant
Bewitching all that commune
With the arcane spirits
In their tumbling abodes

Beneath the gigantic boulders
Worn smooth over infinity

By gravities chaotic commotion,
Fed by the granite permeable
Retentive peaty highland moor
It's spongy mossy surface
Dotted with piercing ancient
Upstanding stony needles
Cavorting, linked together
In subtle supernatural
Telepathic communion.

The Mermaid of Doom

The rocks of Rock cry
Impregnated with the wayward souls
Of seafarers broken at the last.

The Mermaid of Doom
Sings her lilting song of the sea
As she reclines by the Padstow shore.

Enthroned upon her barnacled
Briny strand
Upon the Bar's rocky drift
By the curse of her own demise.

After the perpetual luminous sunset
Spectres of sailors and free-traders
Haunt the towans and
Scabrous slate cliffs.

Face the rock face
Souls carved in anguish cry
To the dulcet
Bar of doom.

The Song of Bucka

Sometimes carried on the wind
From shores along the
Exciting, stimulating
Craggy, rugged and remote cliff tops
Purple, brown and golden
Partially framing
The wild Celtic sea
Sea birds cry, gliding,
Swooping, diving
Murmuring the song of
An archaic discernment
Muted yet melodic;
Lyrical and unusual
Oft unheard but caught
As if unbidden by the seekers
Of the wisdom of the land and sea
Where sea-folk huddle,
Residing in caves
Dark and hidden by briny tide
And cleft shadow

Espied only from above ·
And the song of Bucka
Strangely fills our ears
A lilting uncanny tune
Reminding us of sirens and mermaids
Echoing around the inner realms
The hidden world of nature
Beyond, just beyond our sphere
Where dreams compose the
Delectable, inspirational song
Their tune wistfully decrying
Twisted histories, hidden
Removed, unreal
Like the gales that blow
Through the craggy dark outcrops
Open ended sea caves, blowholes and
Narrow snaking harbours;
The Song of Bucka
Revealing a cultural tune
An ancestral anthem
Weaving past to present and
Clarity to vision.

Tintagel Haven

The acrid saline splatter of
Incoming waves
Sweep over the inky slate
Darkened bulwark
Of the misty headland.
Frothy white moorland water
Cascades into this rounded cove
Running across dark-grey sand
And black sea-pebbles
Concocting
Hydro-alchemical vapours
Which entice and weave their spell ·
Inhaling, we discover
A winding twisting path
Into the gigantic cavernous
Watery lair
Of magic and deception
Where echoes sing
From the distant shores, of
Other spheres

And alternative spaces
This spectral cave of fantastic
Gothic delight
Which turns the bright warm day
Into a cool damp night.
Serpent energy flows through
This space, an eternally
Reconnecting glyph
Spiral dancing gesticulating
With no end or beginning
Beneath the plateau island of
Ancient Kings.

St Clether

Down along the vale of
The sparkling Inney
A holy enclosure lies hidden,
Where Brychan's son constructed
His sanctuary amid
The wild rocky outcrops
And glistening rivulets
Trickling down into the river.
The water chapel of the valley
Exudes its secrets
From the flowing waters
Beneath the sacred altar fine.
Ghostly reliquaries awash,
Add potency for pilgrims
As they drink in the divine
Across centuries
Living history.
A thin place
This sacred divine space
Peaceful and serene

Inspiring the traveler
Creating original blessing
Broadcasting across time
Like a holy benediction
Emblazoned in our hearts.

Tredethy

The beauty of each season
Crown the hills
With inner light
Unpolluted skies allow a
Front seat view
Of the universe
At night.

Arched o'er the river valley
From whence the
Ancient Spirits came
The half-moon beams
Through the mystic trees
Grey slate and granite
Glistens in the rain.

Whispered ghostly secrets
Gently intrude our
Peaceful nights
Echoes 'twixt
Soft rounded hills

By the crooked river,
Silver bright.

The archaic baying of
Cheney's hounds
Down the Georgian chimneys sing,
Brings snow and
Frosty winter's chill
Before the warmer
Climes of Spring

Burst forth anew with
Pulsing life
Upon our ancient Cornish hill,
Tansys Golowan burns
Warm and clear
A fiery beacon for
Old Joan's will.

Our copious tasty harvest
Nature's larder
Bulges tight,
Libations to the
Ancient earth
Whilst the spectral Barn Owl
Hunts at night.

Lines of power flow through
The land, beaming energy
Light and dark,
Pulsing, racing,
Guizing, swirling,
From the love of my
Beating heart.

The Blessing Moon

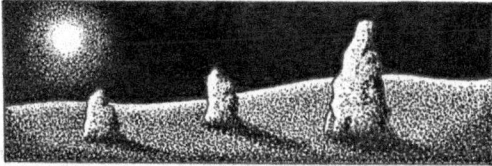

Full moon mysterious misty
Monday on the
Cusp of the mighty moor,
Energy beings are called up dancing
Tides move against the saline shore.

Ancient starlight upon the
Inner realms the Cosmic Inspirer
Seeps and creeps, celestial music
Fills my inner ear, the mermaid's
subtle song lilts and leaps.

Singing, surging, rising and falling
The waves of the bitter sea
Sweeping, cleansing
Healing, soothing
Her soul reaching out to me.

Zennor Quoit

Between craggy hilltop
And Holy Carn
Amongst scrubby gorse
In the midst of steep rolling
Tawny moorland hills
Edged by the vast turmoil
Of the wide stormy Atlantic;
Moor and Sea
Wind and tide
Megalith and horizontal rain
Sky and earth sing a
Desolate solitary tune
From heart of the
Ancestral abode
Deviating through misty movement
Of swirling dancing ghosts
Reaching across the
Invisible spectral gate
Holding, presenting, gesticulating
Through the heart of matter
The hidden splendid realm
Whence we return.

Observations of a Cornish Sunrise

White frost encompasses
The undulating landscape,
Silver moon
Pale amid the morning shines.
Red glow upon the east
Casts a curious light
Demonstrating a warmth promised
Across deep shadowed and
Frosted hills.
The stillness of this winter's scene
Foretells a secret from another age
And a silence that deafens
With its intensity,
Fills my aching heart
With the jewel of this sunrise hour
Which stands alone, eternal,
Amongst the tonal hues
Of the dawn-clad sky.
A planet's Angelic quality

Arouses speculation from the
Devastation of another time!
How many light years
Arise before the star of time and us?
I lift mine eyes up along the line
Of infinity, creating days'
Shadows and features.
Ice-like tendrils claw at me
Breaking the misty heady textures
That betroth thine eyes to me.
O how I wonder
What made this universe creation?
And how I wonder
At this morn-tide hour
How all of this may manifest?
For it is more profound
Than a flock of birds
Alighting at dusk, or
That of a whale that blows
Cascading water aloft
Amid the wild and beautiful seas.
And at this precise second
I feel at peace
With the heartbeat of Nature
Within this wondrous
Contoured and delectable
Peninsular land in which I dwell.

Liminal

The twilight hour fades
Through the russet boughs and
Deep green leaves
Of the ancient
Proudly smooth and strong
Beech tree gateway.
Diminishing light
Pastures sigh, relaxing
Welcoming the dream of night,
Dusken delight.
The hidden realm
Glimpses I have known
Gleaned through
Past enchantments.
Time and space
Back and forth,
Forth and backwards,
Moving at the perimeter of all
Known and unknown things.
The old owl screeches
Her dinner-bell death-cry, whilst
Sacred time collapses into
The past and the future

Of the eternal now.
Ancestors, descendants
Forever engaged by an
Eternal twilight hour.
Whispered incantations,
Heart of hearts, on a
Melding twisted forest shore
A swirling mere of time
In this intangible arena
Among the trees.
Softly-slowly-deeply- darkening
Crepuscular-creeping
Sweet time twixt worlds colliding.
Covert moving shadows
Offer glimpses through the
Deepening darkening dell
Bridging the bridge of
The flowing river across the void
Of bubbling visionary glimpses
Tumultuous, ever-changing
Time merging oneness from
Flowing inspiration,
Transpiring from occluded canyons
Within collective thoughts,
Like mountain ranges, vast and lofty
Echoing the consciousness
Of Nature's Ancient Spirits.

Carn Brea

Clouded shrouded hill of vision
Stark silhouetted luminous beacon
Carn of fire,
Hidden twixt the veil
You speak to me.
Ancient castle
Sprouting from contorted rocks
Perched as though ready to make
A leap of faith
Into the sacred valley below
By the ancient well
With the cure-all waters,
Filtered through ageless strata
Of hill's geology.
Granite, compacted and weathered
Through ages past,
Twisted and sculptured by
Giant's hands
At this mini mountain of madness ·
And high above amid summit's three
Lie secrets of another aeon
Rested and guarded by the
Mysterious midsummer menhir
Keeper of the strange lost heritage
And the landscapes mysteries.

Song of the Stones

Like an invisible network
With solitary antennae
Guarding the ancient past
Keeping secrets.

Identifying
Liminal landscapes
The gateways and signposts
Leading to a mysterious past.

Their ghostly forms
Silently singing the
Perennial wisdom of
The secret terrain.

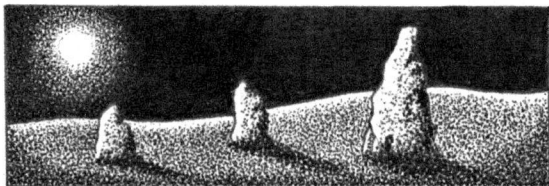

Men Gurta

The towering stone on
The ancient downs
The pulsing land crowned
With archaic mounds
The song of the stones is loudest here
On the biggest hill,
The past feels near.

The Stone of Waiting, standing proud
Its giant form below
The scudding clouds
An old meeting place,
A boundary zone
In a landscape of many
Upright stones.

The vistas of the compass round
The highest moorland hills
To the east, astound
To the north and west,

Lies the rocky shore
In the south, Hensbarrow Beacon
Rises to the fore.

Upon these downs where
Old bones lie
Beneath the earth,
Beneath the sky
Where legend and lore
Is close to see but continues
To remain a mystery.

Also available

Bega and the Sacred Ring

Restoring a Goddess Archetype

Alex Langstone

www.spiritofalbionbooks.co.uk

Coming soon....

From Granite to Sea

*The Folklore of Bodmin Moor and
East Cornwall*

Also available

LUCIFER BRIDGE

ALEX LANGSTONE

www.spiritofalbionbooks.co.uk

Also available

Spirit Chaser
The Quest for Bega
Alex Langstone

www.spiritofalbionbooks.co.uk